BRIEF LIVES

BRIEF LIVES

Poems by
Sonia Gernes

UNIVERSITY OF NOTRE DAME PRESS
NOTRE DAME–LONDON

Copyright © 1981 by
University of Notre Dame Press
Notre Dame, Indiana 46556

Library of Congress Cataloging in Publication Data

Gernes, Sonia.
    Brief lives.

    I. Title.
PS3557.E685B7   811'.54   81-40454
ISBN 0-268-00666-0 (pbk.)   AACR2

Manufactured in the United States of America

*for my parents
and my grandmother, Elizabeth…*

Contents

PRACTICING

Acknowledgments

The author and publisher are grateful to the following publications for permission to reprint:

Argo for "Margins of the Map"

Bitterroot Magazine for "Haworth: For Emily Jane Bronte" and "Birthday Poem: In Michigan"

Cedar Rock for "Back Home in Indiana," "Practicing," and "What I Did This Summer"

College Composition and Communication for "For the P.O.W. in My English Class"

The Colorado Quarterly for "Small Sorrows," "Three Reasons for Leaving," and "Solo"

Florida Quarterly for "Almanac"

Gramercy Review for "Compensation"

Green River Review for "The Priest and the Glass Eye"

Indiana Writes for "Forecasting the Winter" and "Four Novembers: An Aviary"

Madrona for "Storm at Bird Island"

New England Review (vol. 2, autumn 1979) for "Auction"

The New Republic for "To Close a House," reprinted by permission of The New Republic, 1974.

Poetry East/West for "Chuckanut Coast: A Season's End"

Poetry Northwest for "Rope Enough," "Water Witch" "The Bats," "Terminal Paper," "Genus, Species," and "The Chick's Reply to the Obscene Caller"

Seattle Review for "Elizabeth," "Dry December," "Plainsong for an Ordinary Night," and "To Speak a Word of Grief"

The Sewanee Review for "The Commencement," first published in the *Sewanee Review*, 80, #2 (spring 1972). Copyright 1972 by the University of the South. Reprinted with permission of the editor.

Southern Humanities Review for "Moon for My Grandmother's Grand'mère"

The Southern Review for "That Piece of Earth" and "At the End of the Orchard Road"

University of Windsor Review for "Entrance Day" and "Going Back"

ELIZABETH

(1868–1962)

I knew right then I was going to live —
grab life like a gunny sack
they said I was too small to hoist,
and not be picking it up in handfuls.
I told them that — that son and wife
who think because I'm ninety-four and fell
and something snapped besides the pickle jar,
who think I'll let go and die.
And I told that little one too,
winter nights when I had her to myself,
I told her I knew right then when the news came
and my sister only twelve,
stuck like a pig on that Wisconsin farm
of Uncle Jake's. That hired hand, come back
because he knew there'd be harvest cash,
and her home alone from church
with the baby sick. The baby watched
it all, they said, the cash box and
the ripping skirts, and the hog knife
when it struck, and he never touched
a hair on it. They say those young enough
shall live. And I was nine. And I took
my sister's years that never had time
to get the sweetness sucked out of them,
and I used them up and I used mine and
they think because I'm ninety-four
I'm done with it. And they don't know

1

no more than that slip of a girl
when I used to tell her how my sister died,
and how old lady Kressbach got it one night,
who used to run an inn by the Wilson store.
They say he done it with an axe
one night when the corn was all put up
and her notes past due, but they never
knew for sure about the axe
because he burned her to the ground,
and some damn fool — some deputy from town —
was trying to find blood stains when it
all cooled off, and everybody knew that
black skull was split in half in back.
I told her that — that little blonde one
whose cheeks were too pink for her not
to be messing in the rouge and her mother
said she never did, which nobody would believe.

And I told her, and those blue eyes
which she never got from her mother's side
would turn the color of her feedsack dress.
And I'd tell her about Heine Schmich
and how they put him in the State Pen
when he prowled once too often
around a barn with a gas can in his hand.
They figured it was him when the church went,
on account of he worked for Uncle John

and that's who the gas can belonged to,
and everybody knew *he* never done it,
and knew Heine had it in for that young priest,
but not exactly why, because it happened
in the Penance box. And when John's barn
went, there wasn't much doubt no more.
And I told her that, before she run off
and joined the nuns for a spell,
which she hadn't ought to have done,
the last of my blood kin, putting her life
where I couldn't reach it, down some
dark hole likely full of bats and mice,
after she wouldn't even kill the gopher
that was getting my tomato patch,
and I told them that girl was too smart
for her own good, but no, they had to let her
take all the strawberry money out of
the savings account and buy one of them
typewriter things, and sit there
snapping letters on a page that sounded
like peas dropping into an empty pan
which she ought to have been shucking,
not old enough to button her own pants
and making up tales about girls murdered
in the hay, which nobody in their right mind
is going to believe, let alone sit down
and read it out of a book, and I told them

Lord knows where she gets that kind of nonsense
when she could have been helping me
with the raspberry canes and pulling out
the hairs around my mouth that never came
until the liver spots got bad,
like she did before she run off
and there's one life less around here,
which doesn't matter much because I got mine,
and they needn't think because I'm ninety-four
and something broke that I'm any worse
than my wedding clock, even if the face is stained,
when it still gets every minute down,
and I told them:

I know what's mine, by God,
and I'll take it while I live.

that piece of earth

THAT PIECE OF EARTH

i.

Old Mary Phillips had breakfast on the tombstones
when the living were not up; told passersby
it was all the same: she'd breakfast with the dead.
Sunny afternoons we watched her rise

from ditches, a sudden weed, viny baskets
trailing on her arm; found her camped
in our country church, snug as plaster saints,
her dresses hung in the vestry case, dishes

cropped like toadstools on the altar rail.
She denied burning candles, had no key.
Someone else had closeted those sooty stubs,
rearranged the flowers in the Ladies Aid bouquets.

A gaunt gray moth, she could slide through wood,
hover in flames no eye could see. No firebug,
she told them all — that time the sheriff came —
what burned on the altar was a sacred spark;

her body, a barricade, would swell into a stout
sod fence they'd have to cross. She knew
her ground, learned long ago:
through the earth is the way to the flame.

ii.

My friend says you are a messy potter, God.
In her hospital bed she knows
she's been kneaded wrong. Drugs
to slick down her mind, glaze faces
that leer on the bathroom door. The nurse
sees nothing; her children bring posters,
cover the sneer, but she knows it's there.

I say
perhaps the fault's in the clay — or wood
that warped in growing long. Her kind lines
are hewn in a beauty she cannot see. Some things
are in the grain.

iii.

A scorpio, I learn from the charts
My region is water, but that's all wrong.
My father, who knows, would say it's earth.

He believes in the dust we'll return to;
taught us to plow around the slopes
rain strips of topsoil, to grow into the element
he'd conserve. He frowned on playing "ghost"

in the graveyard, petticoats like blight upon our heads.
White was better for daylight. Communion days
or Corpus Christi, farm mules, like heathen,
watched our processions from the fence. Two by two,

we were lilies behind a cross, our petals tossed,
our knees bent for the blessing of the Host.
I knelt one year on my grandfather's grave, my legs
shortened stems, white stockings staining in the sod.

I am the color of that clay turned windward,
those furrows where my father seeks the flame,
says we live by trust, take our seasons knowing
the part that's clay, the hand that goes back to the soil.

THE COMMENCEMENT

i.

At twelve I learned to shoot;
— a country child, a girl
who'd grown with summer's length,
and could be lured, in brittle days of fall,
toward homemade targets
traced in chalk and shoe dye
on discarded barrels near the barn.
There, elbowed clusters
of gangling boys, my brother's friends,
aimed at manhood with their twenty-twos,
and gave not me
but my marksmanship
a grudging nod.

My brother was three-fourths a man
that autumn, as he stalked the farm
almost immune to feverish leaves,
and I stalked in his strides,
not yet a woman
on that fierce fragile border
where the child dies.

Together we tracked the autumn fire
pulsing through our father's woods;
Indian-file,
we kept the path to the third ravine
where gray squirrels cling

to the maple trees
like curious fruit.
Sideways on a massive trunk,
and plump for winter sleep,
one hung, and cocked his head.
His liquid eye
meeting mine through the metal sights
blinked in puzzlement; my finger found
the metal ring.

I did not see him fall.
I did not hear the sound
as my brother's gun
plucked another from an oak.
The shock of rifle wood
against my breast
numbed the bright unknowing
of eyes; shattered the taste
of autumn fire.

ii.

We skinned them on a maple stump
altar-smooth in the raging leaves,
peeling off their hides
— like undressing children,

11

snowsuits welded to their flesh,
like cloth grown into a wound —
pulling and pulling
our arms taut as bone,
our tendons tight with aching,
our eyes strained with sight:
     glossy-membraned flesh,
     the quick knife,
     smoldering mauve of erupting gut,
     the carcass, like an embryo,
     headless in my hand.

My brother carried home the meat;
the tails were mine
(blood-tipped fur leafing from a bloodless stalk):
a trophy,
a virile badge,
a memory, like a tribal band,
to wear and reenact
the ritual of autumn,
the sacrifice.

FORECASTING THE WINTER

Wooly-worms, the only thickness in the grass,
cling to the burial ground, have black stripes
so broad she says the winter will be deep
but not so long as what her husband weathers.

We leave rusting mums to season that sleep
underneath the hickory tree; the squirrels
are nesting lower there than ever in her years.
Even the owls build different dens; they have been

quiet for too long. Last night, she says,
the wind made tramping sounds, siphoned off
the chimney's smoke which settled to the ground.
That kind of cover doesn't warm — it tallies

the days. From the horns of the moon pointing down
she knows how long to wait the snow and when.

She gives me bittersweet and hickory nuts,
a saying she's preserved: "the young can afford
the cold" — the long wind that wrestles in the hearth
but always sleeps alone. I have no gifts,

am ashamed to share unripened words I hoard
against the winter in my skin. I know the signs:
the crickets cry a sort of cold I can't afford. My hair
is heavier this year; I want a home closer down.

ALMANAC

i.

Horses aren't the only thing
Old Hank doctors these days. His shoeing gear
went with the wind that high-corned night
the tornado got his barn. The walleyed cow
lost only her astonished cud, but his prize boar
and chestnut stud rode down glory to the grave.

He reckoned his lightning rods
weren't enough; he's learned to be wary of weather,
studies sunsets, tides, the length of fur
on squirrels come winter.

He looks askance at my garden, says
my seed's not right; buried fish
would make my soil richer; root crops I must plant
in the dark of the moon.

ii.

I plant, but my flashlight should be stronger.
I mix seeds in the dark, press down
on substances I do not know. My hands
feel strange shapes; I was not warned
of the damp earth's pull.

Weeks go by. No leaves appear, but fishlike,
I feel a sinking. I move my bed to the attic,
hang houseplants from the rafters, roof,
lie belly-up as the old moon gnaws its own rind through —
but in the dark, the ground moves closer. The roots
have taken hold.

DRY DECEMBER

for my brother

You raise the ladder on this unnatural winter —
a morning of weak skies and naked grass
where we had thought to find
sun on the Minnesota snow.

In the granary loft, we scoop away
the drifts of twenty winters, tentative;
this chaff is all the mice have left
from a former season's grain.

I pull out first a picture frame;
you move boards from a slotted box of glass.
The player piano's discarded gears
shine on the bottom like a xylophone.

We play back simple years, decisions
filtered like grain through the fanning mill.
Between us, we have left four lives behind.

This winter, when nothing blankets the house,
the alfalfa fields, the paths
we walked away from, we peer
into a tool box, the aluminum tube

of your first fishing rod. We take
them back, claim a piece of the pony hames,
a measure of flax from the coffee can.
I take from the rafters a planter

some great-grandfather held by hand
down furrows of ancestral corn.
Outside, the air clouds again,
frost crystals layer the bridal wreath.

Here,
we tidy the space we've recovered:
you blow dust from the planter,
freeing the hinges, clearing the lines.

ROPE ENOUGH

the hay:

We were the penitentiary's best customer
that year my brothers made the rope machine,
buying bales of its hard-labor twine
to string the sweet loom of our alfalfa field.

A boy at each end, I was the bright bobbin
that coursed between the twisting strands,
blonde hair floating out and out with the running twine,

weaving rope strong enough to rip the flesh
from our father's hand that summer in the mow.
They grafted him in a body cast — a round white cup,
his elbow plastered for the handle's crook.

Looking back, I want to tip him,
pour out the pain that floated to his eyes,
let love by the pulley where he hitched that rope

to rafters in the shed, his own therapy,
pulled and pulled that handle of an arm
back to length and use. Three fates in that field,
we had measured out his pain, his health.

the belt:

> This birthday,
> I learn a sailor's art; tie down
> one by one those strands that slip
> and make my counting wrong.

> > I number back to strokes I've brushed
> > in my mother's hair — white threads
> > that multiply, snap like worms
> > as each part grows. She has seen hours
> > wriggle in the hand, dissolve into parts
> > before they die.

> I pull this partial belt in line,
> leave out the beads my friends advise
> (I don't want what turns). Where string ripples
> I pattern knot after knot, design
> my defense. What I tie
> stays.

the hanging:

> Carol swallowed Mayo Clinic thread
> the weeks her esophagus closed. Hand
> over hand, like fishline, reeling in
> and out again, it was all she had
> against that sealing off.

Nights I wake to feel a closing,
a stricture in whatever goes within,
I hunt for pencils in the dark,
string out words across a page,
filament by filament, testing
until they're strong.
I know the old saying: men given rope . . .
I'm careful enough. I've seen friends
tangle in their words, dangle
where some capricious muse
hoists dreams on attic rafters, smashes
other loves, breathes the peace of oven doors
that open only once.

Wherever there's rope, there is danger;
I keep mine to the size of twine,
know that alone it won't hold me,
but it's there, tangled and dark by the bedside
nights I wake and swallow, swallow, hoping
it is enough.

BACK HOME IN INDIANA

for Ciaran O'Carroll

Were we to love in Indiana,
I would teach you
passions of the landlocked heart.
Groundswells would be swift
but languid. My body would part
from yours and level like a plain
where half-expected roadways curve.
Trucks would hurtle through the night.
The towns, when we came upon them,
would lie prone — sleepers unnerved
by a vast bed, unfiltered light.

                              Love,
far from glen and hawthorne tree,
you would shoulder the air
differently; would learn the trick
of the steady wheel; how to wear the heat
like a canvas glove, running miles
through your fingers like so much wheat.

You would go south
through an alphabet of towns
where children toss voices
from hedge to hedge at dusk;

westward, where Gary's great mouth
tears at the heartland's seams,
spits flame by night, steel by day.
You would learn that searing message well;

at every river's end, the sway
of corn leaves rasps out the dusty swell
of plump barns, well-fed sameness, the husk-
less truth of what we would be.

Were we to love here,
our coming would leave
no cleft in the day. Simple
as sheaves, our limbs would weld
nothing to this tempered land.
We would bed in the forge itself;
we would be the fired clay.

brief lives

PLAINSONG FOR AN ORDINARY NIGHT

The Amish sit down on nights of usual weather,
when nothing is wrong in northern Indiana
and nothing particularly right; when September
settles like a brooding hen, they sit and make
their plain and weekly letters for the *Budget* news:
In Salem, jars and cans are nearly filled with summer,

but the martins left, those busy days, before they knew.
Seed land has opened itself to winter wheat and weather,
and that stray rooster, pecking out the kernel of September
afternoons, will soon end up in the frying pan. Summer
was unkind to muskrats dead upon the road, and Indiana
wants slow-moving signs attached to every buggy made.

Nothing is particularly wrong in northern Indiana,
though Mary Luthy's finger sliced her summer
shorter, and Verna Kropf's grape jars exploded into news.
Mrs. Gabb's son went to drink and never got her coffin
        made . . .
but melons are rounding out the air of late September
the way marigolds flare up and fuel the dying weather's

fumes. Gardens are at the stalling point when summer
goes, but underneath the ground, parsnips swell and new
potatoes are fleshier than one expects in Indiana.
Lately, frosts have made a chaste, austere September,
but tonight, a bright moon shines. Youngfolks make
the most of days that linger. Courting buggies weather

25

ruts that drive older wheels to the shop. That new
horse of Fisher's spooked and skipped the bridge this
        summer;
the new wife had his ankle to soak and cows to milk whether
she liked it or not. The Alymer depot burned September
first; a load of hymnbooks and harness leather made
an unreined fire. And so things go in northern Indiana:

Mose F. Miller, 91, still steps off early September
walks as though morning itself might be something new.
Alma, who would have been 17, died this summer;
a load of bright, sliding hay blotted out the Indiana
sun too long, and her bees, without being told, made
honey dark, but sweet. Crows mourned the cooler weather.

Toward morning, a steady September rain will weather
out the end of summer. Libations of cider will be made.
And the Millers of Goshen, Indiana, will pluck the late beans
        like news!

AUCTION

They are selling my afternoons
stacked up like saucers on the lawn,
my doilies, sewing chest, my coffee pot.

"A fine antique," proclaims the man
with the megaphone face, and the bed
my babes were born in — is gone —

is gone. The heat seams me indoors.
They sell my quilts, what pieces
of flesh and dark I can still recall.

They sell the walnut chest of drawers.
I did not tell them: the mottled mirror
is where the woman lives. I saw her

one twilight, dressed in my wedding face,
with a single jewel I never owned.
Certain nights I rose and could not sleep:

she was Spanish, a duchess, a mermaid,
eyes stippled like a trout stream,
pupils chipped from water and time.

I dared not tell how I floated to join her,
my joints liquid as lamp oil, in a country
far as childhood, a fragrance light as tulle.

27

Now they check for dovetailed corners,
pry at my life for loose veneer.
When the money is counted, they will

load the old lumber of my bones
in a wheelchair, store me in a sterile
lumber room. She will not store so easily.

Once only she spoke, like water
sucking down a stone. "Hush," she said.
"It has been decided. I will not go

when they take you. They will sell
what is solid. I am breath, darkness,
the essence of rain. I am what stays,

do you hear me? I am what remains."

TWO LETTERS

(from letters of Georg Hornung)

i.

Winona, Minnesota
January 1, 1868

Much beloved children:

Yes, time goes — I have to write
the days, the months, the years.
The 63rd year of my age is close
and mother's 62nd.
Leisebeth has, since the end of October,
a little daughter; Christina's family too
is well and cheerful. Their harvest is good:
600 bushels of wheat, and food enough
for people and cattle. Peter builds
a new house; by spring the lumberwork
will soon be ready.

We have a covered farm, no lack
of wood, a house halfway to the water.
Our kitchen and cellar is full, much
cabbage and turnips. We have raised
and killed a good pig of 250 lbs. I make
a good wooden fence; a field of winter
wheat stands wonderful within it.

Only one mishap done last fall:
a prairie fire came and burned a haystack.
Our new neighbor did it — a brother-in-law
to Eva Knapp. He made a fire in his clearing.

Today it starts to snow again a little,
but not cold; we have a sleighing way.
Please let me hear from you.

                              your very loving father

                    ii.

                              Rochester, Minnesota
                              September 2, 1869

Much beloved children:

I am much pleased to hear from you,
especially that the grandchildren write
so beautifully. O my dear ones, you
are inviting me to visit in Ohio. It
would pleasure me much, but the railroad
took so much from me for fifty miles,
how would I stand it for days? And this:
I do not like to leave mother's grave.

I have sold my land: 28 hundred dollars.
The buyer will pay 20 hundred if they build,
next to the cemetery by Philips', a new church.
I do not like to be hard in this matter;
mother and Christina are there.

After I collect in October the remainder
of my money, I consider Ohio. The interest
I give to Joest for the trouble I caused;
I have only to pay the doctor
a hundred more.

News here is not so pleasant:
a man three weeks married, killed by a
Sioux, a board thrown at his chest. 18 miles
from Winona, a baby is missing. Indians
are suspected. The child was alone — the parents
in the field. Weather is hot. Thunderstorms
cause damage on the railroad and crops.

I close now.
This from your loving father, written
with trembling hand. I will not
be able to do much longer.

WATER WITCH

I came to you, old man, out of thirst.
"Here," I said, "is my money. Two
coins that held down my father's eyes,
a penny the lover once slipped
in my shoe. I have nothing more."
You took. You invited me in.
I fear you have deceived me.

You offered choice and I chose:
the forked hickory over the smooth copper wand.
You said: "Twisting down over water,
it will wring skin from you hand." I thought:
It is tradition. Only blood
will regain him. Love must be hard.

I went, as you directed, first to the mill pond.
There he had pulled me from the dance,
his kiss moist as the wheel in the dark.
Next, I paced off his length in the meadow
where we lay. I poised the rod
over his grassy heart, his groin,
the collarbone where my head had rested,
the flowers that grew in the space
I assigned to his brain.

At night,
with eyes closed, I followed rivulets,
waiting for a twitch, a rapid jerking,
a sign to lead me, like a scattered string
of beads, to a pearl, a pulse, the links
within the linking of his blood.

There has been no turning. My hands
grew blistered from the fierceness of my clutch.
Even at the spring where I saw him smile
at one with coal-black eyes, there was not
the slightest pull or twitch.

I came to you in thirst, old man,
and you have deceived me. In the well
of his smiles, another's throat
grows sleek. I have watched her from doorways:
her hands are smooth, on her wrist coins jingle,
beneath her apron when she moves along the street,
I have seen the liquid gleaming
of a copper rod.

CENTIPEDES

They move faster
when nothing else
is on the walls, she says,
and keeps them bare,
a screen, whiter than her sheets,
where she can focus movement anywhere
around the bed.

They breed from nothing she knows,
not intercourse; segments simply
break apart; pieces
climb the ladders in her legs.

She has checked it out,
watched them cross her wrist
like a razor slash. Her text says
they've been known to grow
a hundred and seventeen
segments of trunk,
each one having a pair
of legs; the last pair ends
in poison.

Lately they have changed themselves
to the color of her rug,
hidden in hair on her arms;
pieces dart about the bed like memories
too quick to know.
She has counted the segments
of one dead in the sheets:
the first for the man
who stroked her as a child, two
for that chapped red-haired boy,
three for the stranger who followed her home . . .

No, she cannot leave this afternoon,
would not think to go;
they split too fast
when she isn't watching,
drop segments
as a train drops cars —
(uncoupling, he called it
the day before he left —
she knew it would happen;
bathing that night,
she'd seen tracks
split across the steam).

Be careful on the steps, she says,
ripe ones crack in corners
and that's where things get lost.
"You're careless with keys," she says;
she's dreamed about a lover
I couldn't hold.

I hold with truth
but the encyclopedia
says a hundred seventeen.
In my own white room,
something catches on the corner of my sleep:
a noise from the street, perhaps,
the scratch above my bed,
a scar on the wall —
but moving.

MARGINS OF THE MAP

> "The writers crowd the countries of
> which they know nothing into the far-
> thest margin of their maps. . . . All
> beyond this is portentous and fabulous,
> inhabited by poets and mythologers,
> and there is nothing true or certain."
> —Plutarch, "Life of Theseus"

I was seven
when they made me learn the names
of oceans, continents, colored shapes
like boots and fists, and fat split plums
tossed into the sea. I traced inlets green
as a lost mother's eyes.

          "Here," they said,
"you shall live. Here is your bed —
(this white tablet standing gravely in a row).
Here is your desk, your bowl, the orphan's prayer
to be said in unison. All days are charted.
Here you will save your soul."

At seventeen, they showed me
to the parlor where he sat. "We will take
one horse," he said. "Salt for preserving
and an iron pot. There may be wolves. And cold.
It is known there are rivers there.
All else is beyond the markings of the map."

"I have no dowry," I said, "not a dish
I can call my own." "The sky
will be a deep new bowl," he said,
"your mouth a cup."
I said: "I will go."

High in mountains, he pulled the cloth
from my own small peaks, taught me crevasse
and hidden canyon — a joyous plunge to silky lakes
my body did not know. On awesome plains,
he rose, and blood swept through me
like the wind through rising grain. I vowed
the land was ours; began to swell with seed.
I said, "We will mark this place,"
but his eyes looked past me through the fire, marked
small eyes that began to circle and shine.

I remember nothing
of when it started. Both of us ate the meat,
drank deeply from streams. His breath grew hotter
in the night; he threw off clothes, returned
too late from hunts; I would awake
to fire in the night. I would call
but his fired eyes would not be seeking mine.

We moved always to newer lands,
shaggy as his face. Soon he would not drink;
words came out in foam. The last night,
wolves gathered, circled thrice. He rose,
pierced their circle with a single thrust,
and raised his snout like a border line.

Now the howling is done. I have burned
the old map. I make new lines while a round moon
traces how my belly swells, new promontory
on the body's well-tracted land. If I live
and this child lives, we shall leave records
before going on.

You who read this,
will have come as far as we have gone.
You will have crossed the boundary of certainty.
You will be walking the plane
that we have walked. Here,
all that is
is true.

ANNIE FARMINGTON'S VERTIGO PILLS

I tell you, it's no fun falling down crazy,
like a backwater drunk, just because some little bones,
three to be exact, halfway inside the brain,
have set up some sort of jig, a regular *Mr.* Bones,
Annie says, playing spoons on his knee inside your head.
Not that you hear it, of course,
but the floor comes up and smacks your nose,
and then you've got *more* bones grinding.

Some says it's water, a regular little dropsy
sloshing through the barrel to the drum,
but Annie, in one of her spells, says it's the bones:
    I'm ruled by a stirrup,
    but it's not a lover that rides.
    Nothing gets forged,
    nothing hammered home.
Said that herself the time it come on her
in the cabbage patch, and those hollyhocks
looked like twirling breasts when she was going down.
Said it just come to her, and she wrote it right down,
soon as she could get up out of the broccoli.

And that girl, the one in here the other day
with the mote in her eye, said it feels like that —
your head all layered like a cabbage
and something pulls some of the leaves,
which shifts, and the others don't,
and the body don't know which ones to lean to.

You ever seen a mote like that,
just cut right out of the blue part,
like a piece of mincemeat pie?
Said it never kept her from nothing.
She could always see the floor
when it was coming up to get her . . .
But I noticed she didn't have no wedding rings,
And those hands just got to fluttering
when she said it was nothing she done
that brought on the attacks. Makes you think
something is out of kilter. Bad as that
little Jeeter girl with the big loose hands;
got into playing with herself and never been right
since. Not that I'm saying that's what brings it on!
Lord knows, Bertie Miller when she come in here
after that miscarriage last month
has her hands full with Melvin. Annie'd say
people like that oughtn't to have the pills —
better dizzy than hiked up again
when there's ten at home and her half into the change.
Takes more than pills to keep some folks steady.

But Annie'd know what your problem is;
she'd say:
        It spins you round,
        winds you up and
        leaves you unwound!
Was going to put that right on the bottles
but the printing cost too much.

Whatever is bringing on your particular case,
I don't think you said yet, I bet
it leaves you cockeyed — hand don't hit the doorknob,
and no sure foot in the dark. It's the bones
for sure. A fellow up here last week —
never seen him before and he didn't buy a thing —
but he says:
     Well, well
     double, double, toil and trouble,
     the anvil's hot, the hammer beats,
     and the cauldron bubbles.
That's what he says, and I says
Annie just wants to keep things in balance,
that's all, keep those bones from pounding on the drum.
And he laughs, sort of, and says:
     A drum, a drum,
     Something crooked
     this way comes.
Said it was right out of Shakespeare.
Can you beat that? And all about the bones!

Now, what was it you were saying
brought your trouble on?

ENTRANCE DAY

i.

Ten years ago
I rode these river hills too fast
in rain my mother
thought would cause an accident,
driving to demand whatever lay
behind the high and cloistered walls.

All of us were calm; my father
just forgot his wallet, brother retold jokes.
My mind numbed itself
on items from the clothing list:

    a metal trunk from Sears
    a laundry bag
    seven bars of soap
    nylons (black) in boxes
    plain stationery, pins . . .

ii.

Sister Mira let us in;
stone like great veined mirrors
watched our steps. A nameless nun
fluttered with the bags, our wraps, her scapular
(My brother said, "How *do* they get those things
around their heads?"), ushered us
through parlors other families occupied
like frightened troops. A Nebraska girl,
sheep-eyed and grinning out her fear,
picked handles on her purse to shreds.

The rest was quick:
they fed the families pie, packed
us off to fitting rooms ("Postulants
wear garb modest, ample, plain . . .")
collected money, makeup, cigarettes,
sent us out to say goodbye.

The family left; I did not cry.
I read *Pax et Bonum* high in stone.
A novice said, "That's peace and good."

iii.

      At evening prayer
behind the novice rows, white-veiled
and straight as laundry pins,
silence was the final cloister door. I felt it
as I feel autumn, tangy and breathing smoke,
pull me out of summer,

                and I feel it now —
a counterpull to flesh. I ride in rain
the glazed green summer of these river hills
and I do not touch. It is as though

anchorites bend to touch the sand
in the scorched, restless autumn of my bones.

THE BATS

That houseful of nuns had no belfries
but fourth-floor attic eaves were close enough
to deliver baby squirrels in spring and bats
in any weather. Summer nights

we stoked our silence with the humid air,
waited for the first barrage of slamming doors
to see nightgowned nuns arise with brooms —
ghosts of crusades past — brandish dust mops,

night-veils, books, exorcise with backhand strokes
the winging dark. A fat nun says
tennis rackets make the surest hit
(Superior says a frying pan); I know

my mettle — I hide; conjure thoughts
of the nun who woke, black wings
inching up her chest. (One gray and furry dawn
two were in the pocket of her robe.)

I don't buy that business of "harmless
mice with wings." I've had gargoyle faces
swoop through my transom as I'm stuffing
rugs in the door. I don't like darkness
zeroing in.

I fear some night in dreams
I'll take to the streets, wing out my mantle
and fly. One never knows what caves
lurk high in bat-lined dark. Those quivering walls
are close. I feel a draft within.

GOING BACK

I am packing my coifed misgivings,
my certainties shorn short as hair
I veiled in black for seven years.
I stuff psalters in with curlers, shoes;
I am going back.

Nun, student,
alone in Seattle three years,
all night I pack in dreams,
rule books hanging like a mobile from my light.
Strange rites that were familiar once
are strange again, and yet are mine —
I want to go. I clutch old friends, faces
about me for habit, cincture my hopes,
gird in my fears.

Waking voices chant softly in my brain;
I remember the words, lean into their sound.

SMALL SORROWS

You have stapled everything down.
Steady and weighted, your houseboat floats
a bay of minor discontent.
The waves will not dislodge you.
You keep pain dampened
down beneath the floorboards,
lone nights pared to a sabre's width.
You say sizing's the secret:
keep things to scale.

Bayonets that stud your walls
tell the story: Pearl Harbor
caught us napping; old cavalry swords
were soon ground down; the new war's
issue made a quicker point — no need
to waste that length of steel
when less and less would kill.

Keep things to size and stapled,
you say as the night floats in.
You're a man who's done it —
when the red-haired wife drifted off
you nailed down a deck, a view.

Hammer in hand, you rule off darkness,
give me reasons for avoiding sorrow.
To keep things even, I counter with rhyme:

Some things do not come in sizes:
the warping of wood your hands laid,
the shift of light within a room,
these earlier, textured twilights,
sudden longing, sadness at noon.

THE PRIEST AND THE GLASS EYE

i.

For 1¢ you would show them
all he saw: the glass eye your father
plucked out when napping, examined with the good eye,
kept in the bureau drawer. At six,
you made it a business: supplying vision
to the neighborhood. You charged a penny a peek
and quiet on the stairs. The day it broke
determined you: the splinters in the hallway,
the running feet, your father's voice: "Who's
there?"

ii.

Now he does not speak. You put your hand
to the paralyzed side of his smile, adjust
the bedrails, wipe his face while
hands shape splintered words.

With one eye and no voice he has
talked with life, watched death ride up,
pass by. You who peddle light,
put a penny in your hand. Listen
to what he sees.

HAWORTH: FOR EMILY JANE BRONTE

Trees lashed the gravestones green
that day at the parsonage windows
and each view was the same: a mouth
of stones, a froth of trees,
and that closing throat of sky.

Out beyond the glass,
wind caught in my slicker,
sailed me across that moor and back.
There was no need to go further.

Down streets cobbled with leaves
torn green and flowing like rain,
I could believe in fluid souls —
in clouds that are not shape but strength,
that dip to skim the moor's edge,
swift in their uncharted course,
voracious and pale, mutinous,
never flying a hallowed flag,
never dropping anchor.

FOR THE P.O.W. IN MY ENGLISH CLASS

The images ricochet.
In the third row, you are not safe
from Sartre's firing squad. The trial held
has said we all must die. I offer flowers
from the Judas tree. The flowers turn to poppies,
their slashes into blood. I am the first
to confess my crime: I didn't know that you would come:
I have mined the room with my reading list.

You come with the others across that field,
make it look easy when nothing explodes —
(You've dodged things before; your timing is good.)
Like Hemingway trout, you steady yourself
in this flow of words, take with the current
those burnt-out years, the trees, the blossoms,
the swamp you know too well to fear.

Lieutenant, your journal opens
like a flower torn in half. Words drop;
the stamen, petals split. In this zone,
it doesn't matter if the pollen burns my skin.
I am looking for what holds us both to earth;
I am looking for a root, a stem.

TERMINAL PAPER

The professor has died in my dream.
We huddle, forms without content,
in the room that was his class,
speak softly, wonder what it was —
enjambment of the breath,
a dissociation of the spirit and the sense . . .
We say nothing correlates.

The wife comes. A net of weeping
curbs her rhythmic stride. She says,
"It came so suddenly. He's dead, you know,
from an infection he picked up
using the Oxford English Dictionary —
that awful O.E.D."

We nod, know how it is,
mutter so she cannot hear:
That's what it gets you, all that
dark research. Surely there's a lesson here.

We fumble in our bags, draw out
clean white cards. We make a note
of that.

MOON FOR MY GRANDMOTHER'S *GRAND'MÈRE*

They did not
even list your name — those fathers
of my father who inked out my heritage,
naming sons and husbands, an issue
of farmers, not poets, on those blank Bible leaves.

But I have pieced you out; have made
you a name from the stirring in my blood,
a face from words that roam like cattle
through my sleep. When the moon has pulled
at my body, I have known you well.

Bred to breed sons for the plow,
you slipped that harness one winter night
halfway from barn to milkhouse; flung out
your pails where the moon touched the snow;

oblivious of night, his arms, of the babes
who sucked you dry, you whirled in that foam,
caught the white spray full on your full-mouthed face,
murmured, "Soul, O my soul!" to the moon.

practicing

PRACTICING

To sign for a single passport
is one way to begin. To take
any journey alone. To be the one
who finds the body on the beach,
eyes splintered like the agate chips
that will wrap around the neck
of every dream. These are ways of practicing.

To walk through autumn without love,
to count in spring what has winter-killed,
to rejoice in late flowers,
dried fruit. In strange countries,
to peer into the boiling pot and watch
dark hands take the turtle from the shell;
to choose the suit for the burial.

The rest are simpler ways:
to lie back as a woman lies
awash in the bedclothes with love —
to feel the bouy of self
slip far from the hand; to trust
the blackness before the surgeon's knife,
colors fleeing like birds
in summer's wake. To step into a storm
and give freely of your breath
for every breath the wind will take.

These are the trial runs.
When the great lightness comes
like a door opening out of the body
or a core falling, swift and aglow,
you will be ready to bite down hard.
You will remember all that has left you.
And then you will go.

BIRTHDAY POEM: IN MICHIGAN

We have flattened out the narrow sun
on this November pier. We pick
late berries, deserted shells —
all that is left of the season.
Your gift is a milkweed pod,
my birthday flower. Its wings
shoot back like a bird's;
this is the time of migration.

When you go, the pier will stop
this ancient creaking. The old rowboat
will be soldered to the shore.
I will watch
the last plank of light lie back.
I will know
when the lake surrenders.

GENUS, SPECIES

This was a love we could classify.
Sure of order, we put our meetings
into phylums, knew what flowered
in our lust. We cited Latin names
for every leaf you photographed, identified
our shells, our claws, the second skin
each day was breathing under.

What was it that we magnified?
Some glacial bloom? Some tissue
sensitive to light — the bright
meeting of eyes upon a slide?

Dark now,
I find no label for your leaving,
wrap the clean sleeve of strangeness
around what skeleton remains. Poor biologist,
I cannot tally my loose fingers,
cannot even name
this lost incessant beast
that paws and paces, raging
the soft cave
my breasts enclose.

FOUR NOVEMBERS: AN AVIARY

i.

Each birthday
something of you flies in.
First, it is a lakeside song,
your fingers waking like wings
against my face;
then, at dusk,
a piece of wood
I stoop to toss
from the parking lot:
it is a carrier pigeon
grave and dying.

Next morning,
fog.

ii.

I return from the airport
to a starling down the chimney,
roosting on the drapery rod,
rapping, tapping at my chamber door.
His eye alone will stir the dust,
tangle the wisps of my hair.

He has one song:
    a winged thing
      breaks whatever holds it
        evermore.

iii.

The snowy owl
can see all of Chicago
without changing perch.
The head pivots
on the bearings of his eyes.
He knows there is no one beside me.
I believe he has no past,
no neck,
no bone.

iv.

The end when it comes
is often in a letter.
I visit the friend
whose brain nestles tumors,
read the numbers
on the bandage round her head.
She is dated like a package,
a postmark that says
she can never return.

Home through the park,
I give your letter
to whatever wind will take it.
November has no birds.
I watch the pieces sail.

CHUCKANUT COAST: A SEASON'S END

On the promontory, spaced apart,
we watch a single duck
separate her grayness from the fog.
You tell me, in November water
she too is stone.

Your voice, our sunless shadow,
cannot sound the fog. We have guessed
and missed each island;
there are no more common seas.

The duck moves with the movement of water.
Between us waves are silent;
water levels into slate.

COMPENSATION

The tests say I hear in one dimension.
My left ear useless as a slug, I've learned to plot
direction, depth; hold the flat sounds
that hold me up. Feeling as the blind feel,
I caress tones with a single ear, nose
the underflow, watch my fingers ripen.

It is the same in love.
When your words have neither depth nor breadth
I round them out, give them shape
with muscle from your arm, know, in silence,
you console yourself because my eyes are blue.
It is a two-planed truce
we are keeping.

A woman friend, thumb bent wrong for the cello,
now plays with words. Winter nights
she dreams she can reach through the fire,
write in cyphers cryptic as flame.
Her unsinged arm draws spheres that reach
the fourth dimension. That, love,
is where I would be.

AT THE END OF THE ORCHARD ROAD:
FOR MARY BETH

"Franciscan Nuns to Sell
70 Acres of Convent
Grounds and Orchard"
Rochester Post-Bulletin

Now the October moon
is all that ripens in the wild plums.

Our windfalls picked,
our hard grapes gathered,
we are the road's last turning
in this bend of oak.

The Vesper bell, that old tolling,
sounds while monarch butterflies
colonize these branches for the night.
Their folded wings are our own dark leafing —

a silence layered with motion and calm.
We cannot tell the wind from their breathing;
when one wing blinks an eye of color
a hundred colors wake to flame.

Travelers, we migrate in our own long thoughts.
When we move, we move together;
we take the wind, the breath, the wings of that tree.

TO SPEAK A WORD OF GRIEF

(for A. K. O.)

I said nothing when your death
came in the mail. Waves
that would not hold you
floated through telephone cords
and washed my rooms with a quiet
so stiff it might have been
your hand. Seven months are gone.

Now I push north through Michigan
knowing that you chose to die. Leaves
raise their veins to a splendid knife;
tendrils stiffen; rain waits in the west.
A friend has written you a letter;
it returns postmarked: low tide.

"I have written to a dead man," he says,
like the chorus to a song. "I have
written to a dead man," plays louder
than the radio, plasters the billboards
of these small towns, shines from the stands
of roadside fruit.

I am writing to a dead man, I say
as Michigan vineyards die leaf by leaf.
I have not forgiven the words
you did not harvest, the small, hard
grapes you pitched into the sea.
To speak of love would be to swallow
all that silence — that gathering
of water, pain and fruit.

I bless/curse these syllables
you left me. My mouth bells
like a hollyhock. These words
will no longer wait.

STORM AT BIRD ISLAND

Resorts close swiftly on the island's beach;
dying lawns, debris, an empty birdbath
sketch out the end of summer, the death
that blasts old leaves against our windowpane.
We pile summer into boxes, load the car in rain.

In June our laughter was an easy, agile prose;
at summer's end we are saved from speech by thunder;
what matter which of us forgot the words, the tinder —
the fire's out. The damp ignition sputters miserably.
Above, low lightning splinters down the dark.

THREE REASONS FOR LEAVING

"a stone, a leaf, an unfound door . . ."
—Thomas Wolfe

i.

The stone
you gave to me, saying,
Do not cast it. Warm from your hand,
it's been ballast in my pocket, weight
for the balance I'm likely to lose.

Some nights I've longed to hurl it;
stand outside myself and pitch rock
after rock where your image rims my eyes,
shatter what lights I have burning,
be my own dark.

ii.

The leaf I've turned over often —
in love as in logic, nothing is new.
I make syllogisms instead of supper:
        if these veins are a rib cage
        and the ribs are flat
        then something's gone.

"Nonsense," you say, and snap shut
your eyes. "It's veins and ribs;
you know nothing
of separate systems."

Sir,
behind your flat black eyes
small veins pulse out
and circle into ribs. What moves
at the back of the eye
is red.

iii.

When locked out, I told you,
there was always the cellar:
old boards to scrape the silence, potatoes
shooting long eyes in the dark.
It was the descent into dampness
in the first home, that father's house;
what mattered was the getting in.

I tend toward doors
that are secret: moss
grips with tiny fingers, old bottled things
loosen in me still. We too have a door,
swept, above ground. Nothing is likely
to grow there. Such traffic we've been making —
one of us wanting out,
the other in.

SOLO

(for Joan Stone)

It's not really a journey —
this staying aloft — what I want
is to sight the terrain. Mornings
when the fog lifts, I see raindrops
bounce one by one on the drugstore roof,
wrap meat in single portions, clean
the flat I keep alone.

Last night at the theatre
I was the intermission — caught
between acts with no one on stage.
Out along Broadway, strangers steered me
to a glassed-in phone, I looked
for familiar signals, but
strangers taxied me home.

On streets so dark I wouldn't walk,
hills rose in banks and I knew
I'd not touched down. I adjusted
my gear, pulled back
to clear the trees. They tell me
black is the color of lonely skies
and I know what I've been learning.
I choose to take my chances
on the lightening dark. For now,
there's nowhere I want to land.

WHAT I DID THIS SUMMER

(an essay in two parts)

i.

I foreswore love for the season;
there is less to regret in domesticity.
Lone and lazy, I kept a reasonable

house, stripped old paint from various
limbs (a sluggish brew), made designs
on the future of my cane-bottom chairs.

I hauled down the trunk my past was shipped
in, tried to remember my former names.
To reduce clutter, I ground up the news, chipped

daily deaths and marriages, old dog-earred
wars, into a pure gray pulp, a bone-
clean sheet on which to bed my rumpled fears.

In short, I slept alone.

ii.

I relaxed. All that remained was to nail
down this peace. But plants I put out
to summer came back matted, full of snails.

My prize butterfly was attacked by moths;
a soft, slow worm bred in the windows
of its wings, a destruction tender as cloth.

Now the twilights all come earlier. They make
sequins of paint peeling from the porch.
Like the way you kissed my thumbnail, I thought.

That was my first mistake.

THE CHICK'S REPLY
TO THE OBSCENE CALLER

What you do not know, my friend,
is that I grew chirping to my present form
on a poultry farm. A fledgling myself,
I could clip wings, pluck banty breasts,
preside at mysteries of the chopping block.
I knew what chickens would be nesting.

There were also ducks and geese.
My mother taught me different tones of quack,
made sauce for the gander, dressed
out the drake. She knew
which rooster's comb to trim, who laid
the rubber eggs, what hen
would cackle loudest. Ah friend,
how she could have taught you
the possibilities
of being fowl.

TO CLOSE A HOUSE

(for C. H.)

To close a house
is to be more sure of distance;
to measure off the days we did not count,
the length of rugs, of ivy vines, the tensile strength
of words that form the linkage we have left.

We have packed and shipped what's over.
Your goldfish swim in their traveling pail,
the phone in a disordered sleep. Disconnected thoughts
pull in and out; I have turned off the gas;
the bills are paid; the clock

ticks off the space I've yet to move in.
Like a child, I try to adjust my pulse,
my breathing. I say your name
in the rhythm of its beat. A last time
I turn the kitchen faucet. The old leak
still gathers — a globe that forms and falls.
I wait to see it shatter, but the water holds,
the ticking holds; I cannot hear my heart.

The house is closed and I must be the mover,
the pendulum that changes space to time.
I breathe and hunt a span to hold me.
I move my hands;
I start the clock.